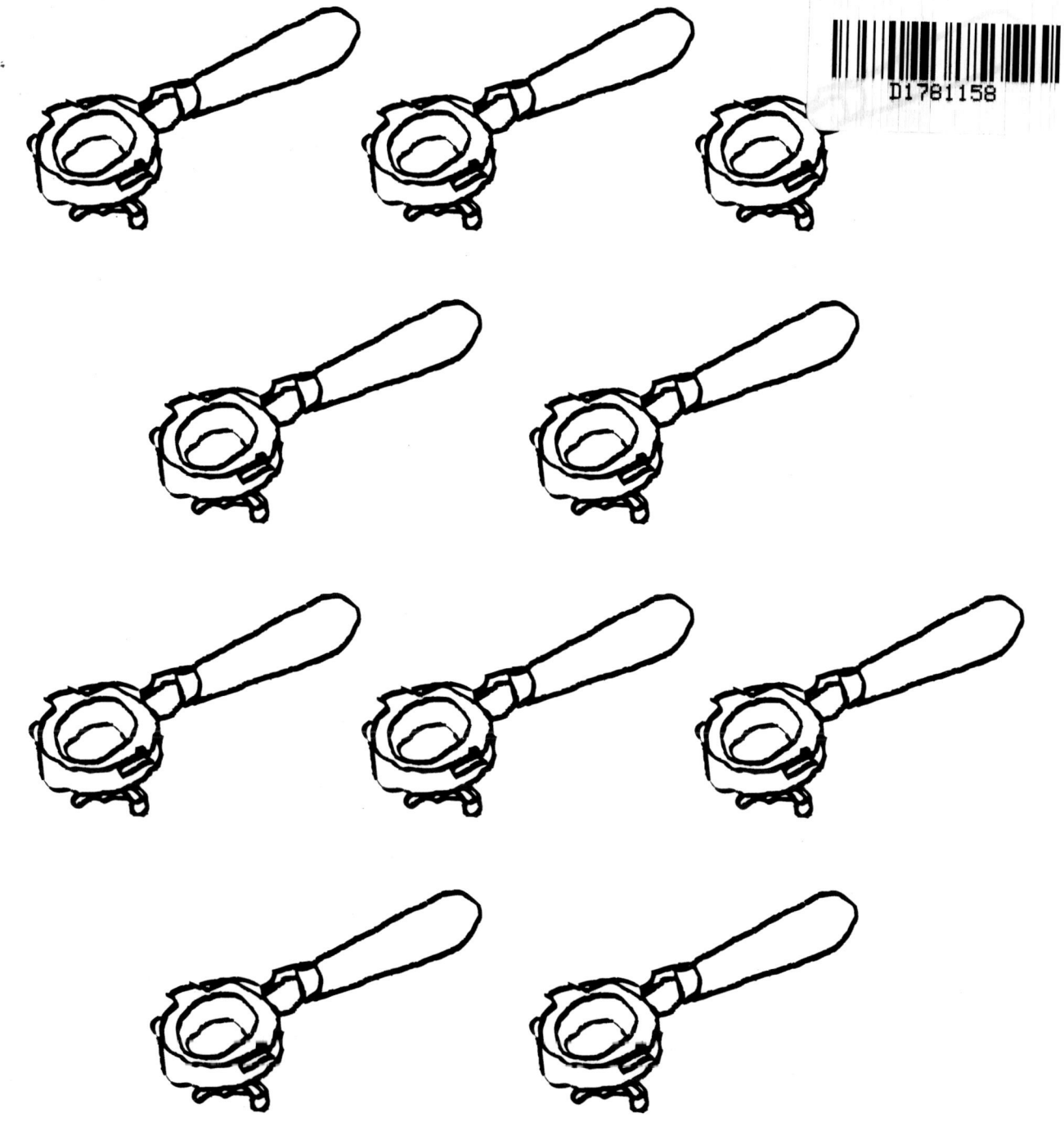

To Meli, Nico and Joaquín
I love you.

In memory of Marco Antonio
You gave your life doing what you loved.
More than a friend, you are my brother.

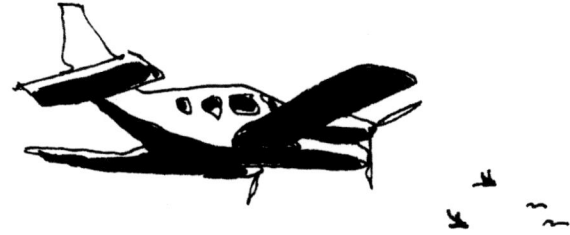

Café on my coffee
Melbourne
An illustrated journey through Melbourne's coffee culture

Copyright © 2019 by Julio Brenes
All rights reserved. This book or any portion thereof may not be reproduced or used
in any manner whatsoever without the express written permission of the publisher
except for the use of brief quotations in a book review.

None of the content on this book was published in exchange for payment by
commercial parties or businesses. Julio Brenes selected all included work.

First Printing, 2019

ISBN 978-0-6484612-1-0

Published by Drawthatout
Prahran, Victoria
3181 Australia
www.drawthatout.com

Concepts and Art direction, Julio Brenes and Melissa Mena
All design, drawings images and photos in this book are done by
Julio A. Brenes Bolaños, unless noticed otherwise.
Text and Stories by real coffee drinkers in Melbourne, Australia.

Acknowledgements
I would like to thank Angela, Evelyn, Janice, Kym and the Melbourne Urban Sketchers
for dragging me around to sketch, you guys are my friends.
Angela Williams for the book idea and ongoing support.
Akiko Bamba, Ariana Callejas for their friendship and acute graphic design eye.
Naomi Watts for proofreading the book and past collaborations, I really enjoed them.
Steven Raspanti, for your invaluable support. We are so fortunate to call you family.
Viet Truong for letting me use his cameras and studio.
My sister Andrea for her professional marketing input and guidance.
My grandfather Victor Julio for his gentleman's example.
My parents and sisters who I love deeply. Thank you for your encouragement.
My wife and her patience. She is my favourite coffee partner.
All the coffee shops in Melbourne for letting me stick around longer than usual.
All the coffee lovers who happily shared their stories. You know who you are. Thank you.
Thank you God, for I can reach you through drawing.

If you wish to participate in future editions of Cafe on my Coffee or order copies of the book,
visit www.drawthatout.com

Cafe on my coffee

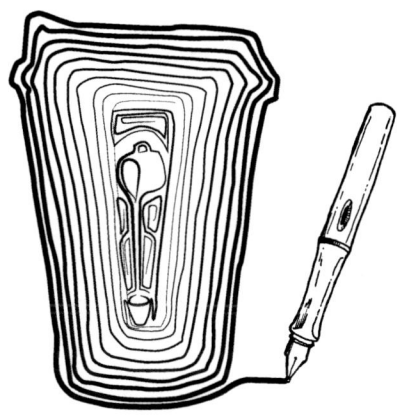

An illustrated journey through Melbourne's Coffee Culture

Julio Brenes

Melbourne (lots of coffee!)

1. Catch the tram

Melbourne CBD area. During lunch break I would catch the tram to meet a friend or rush to a coffee shop I wanted to draw

2. Cycle to a gig

Coffee shops from the Fitzroy, Collingwood, North Melbourne surrounding areas. Our friends would meet us for afternoon coffee and then cycle to a music gig.

3. Drop by the market

We would drop by Prahran or South Melbourne markets right before our mourning coffee.

4. It's not far off

meaning great coffee shops outside our usual hang out suburbs.

scan me!

Melbourne
AUSTRALIA

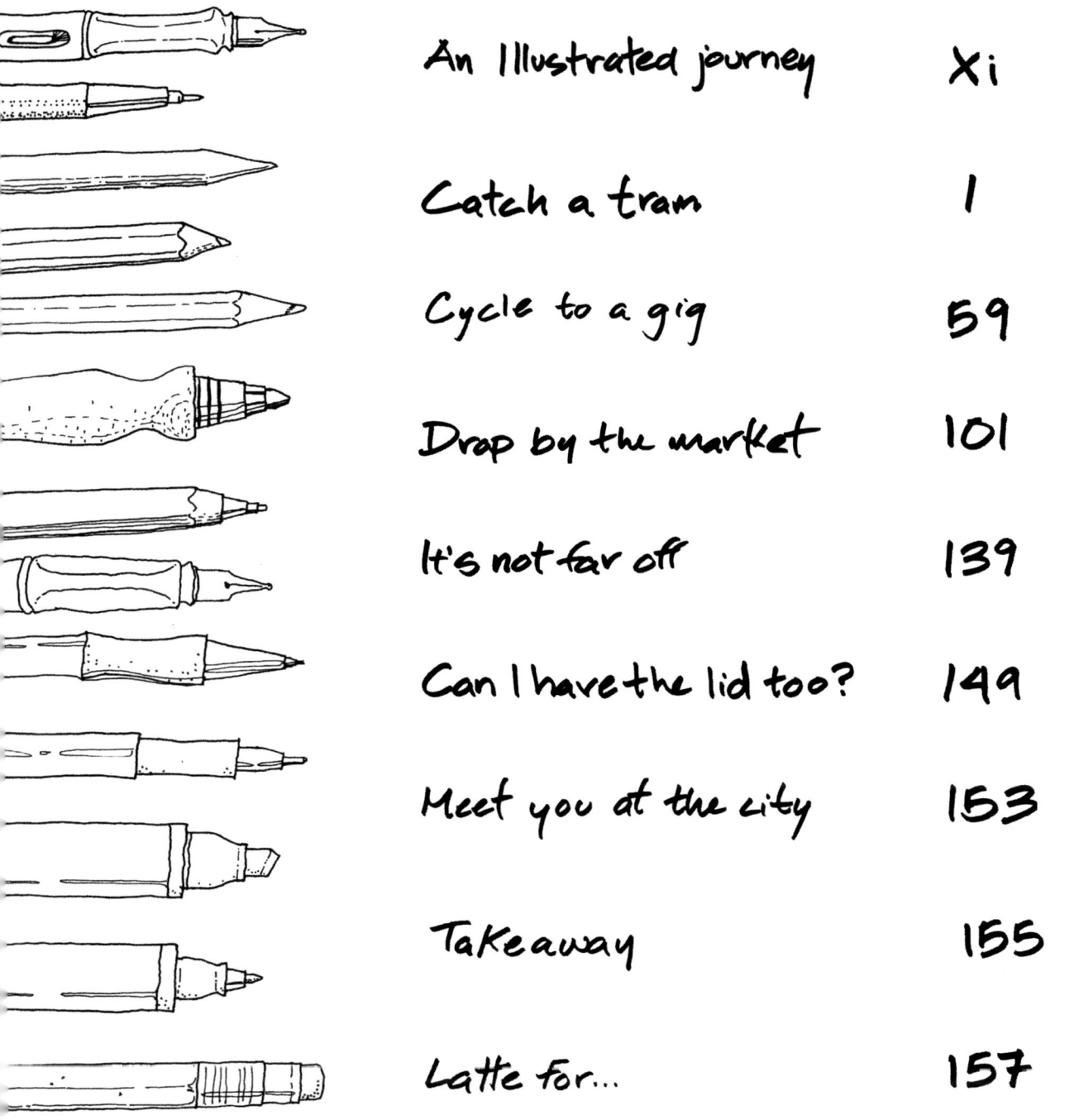

An Illustrated journey	xi
Catch a tram	1
Cycle to a gig	59
Drop by the market	101
It's not far off	139
Can I have the lid too?	149
Meet you at the city	153
Takeaway	155
Latte for...	157

"Happines is a good book"
Charles M. Schulz

"Happiness is a cup of coffee and a good book"
Unknown

"Happiness is drawing having coffee while making a book"
The author

An Illustrated journey

Introduction by the Artist
April 2018
Melbourne, Australia

I've always loved listening to stories. When I was a kid growing up in Costa Rica, taking the bus from one destination to another I always ended up chating to the stranger next to me.

It felt as if life itself was speaking to me, when to be grateful, when to be careful, when to worry, and when to let go. . How I should work hard to achieve what I want. My random encounters on the bus gave me a window to many stories… only to be cut short by our arrival at the next stop. I learned to be present.

Now to sketching. When I sketch it feels like meditation. The act of drawing imprints a moment on my memory and I remember every detail. The weather, the light, the sounds, the textures, the conversations, the aroma of coffee beans. I remember the start of the drawing and the movement around me whilst I silently capture the impression in front of my eyes. Time stands still.

The paper cup is an ideal surface for the ink. The warmth of the cup in my fingers and on my lips is so comforting on a cool, winter's day. Sketching these cafes on my coffee has prompted many interesting conversations, and the challenge of sketching on a curved surface adds to the joy.

Melbourne is renowned for its love of coffee and art, and by blending these two loves I feel a part of the fabric of the city. This book is an exposé of my favourite cafes in this great metropolis. To the coffee lover, I'm sure you'll recognise a familiar haunt! To the sketching aficionado, I hope these pages bring you inspiration. They reflect countless hours of coffee drinking while pondering the stories of those people who have made Melbourne's cafes their caffeine sanctuaries!

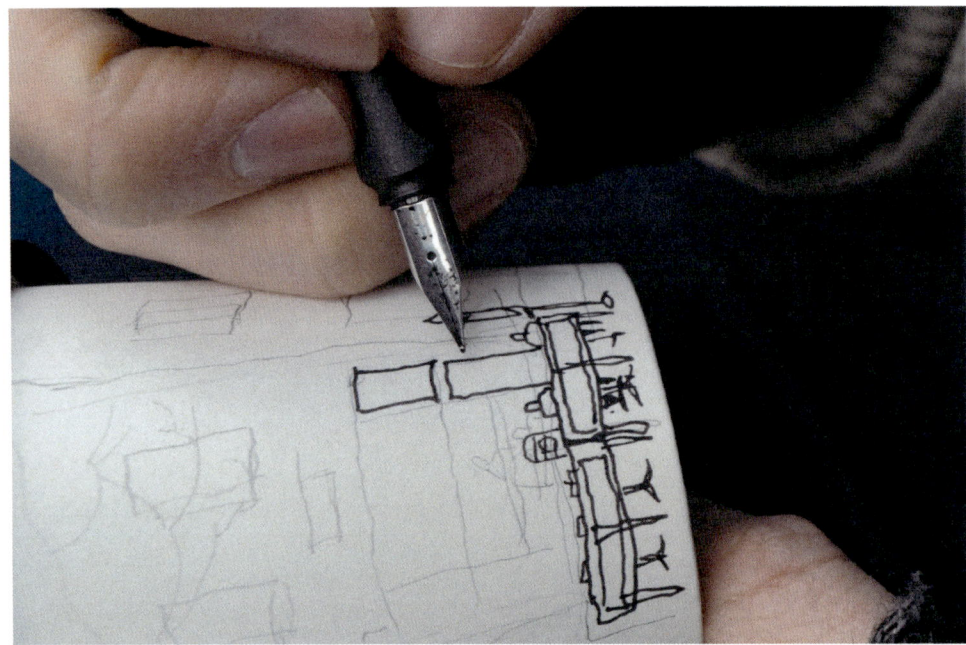
Sitting on a kerb on Gertrude Street, drawing Archies after ordering a latte.

This book is an illustrated journey through Melbourne's cafes with reflections from the regulars who frequent them.

I hope you enjoy my gift to a city that loves coffee, art, and storytelling.

Julio Brenes
Latte, no sugar.

Author and Artist 2018
Melbourne, Australia

I find Melbourne's climb to Livability remarkably fascinating. How a central district once forgotten was injected with life through urban planning and how the cafe experience is partly responsible for this.

Catch the tram

The little Mule Cafe
Melbourne CBD

"This cafe in Melbourne is pretty secluded - that's why I like it. It's quiet, the coffee is good, and the staff are lovely. I can sit here in the sun and eat my lunch... can't really do that anywhere else."

Jordan, 22
Strong latte

The Switchboard
Melbourne CBD

"When customers come up and genuinely appreciate the coffee that we do, and they are really thankful for it. That for me is the most heartwarming. It makes me feel very happy!."

Claire (Barista)
Iced latte

Brioche by Phillip
Melbourne CBD

"I come here every morning. Coffee is good and I used to love their doughnuts but I don't have them anymore, mainly because I am trying to lose weight."

David
Skinny latte

Seedling Cafe
Melbourne CBD

"I'm on my way to the office, I don't have time for breakfast and my 2 year old woke me at 5am. This is going to get me into the right frame of mind and give me the energy and clarity I need for an important client presentation."

Olivia, 41
Bulletproof

8 Cafe on my coffee

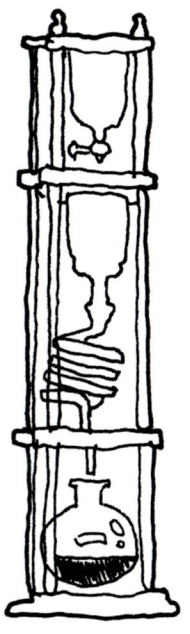

Chapter House Coffee
Melbourne CBD

"Tucked under the archways of St Paul's Cathedral, Chapter House Coffee typifies Melbourne's laneway coffee culture. This boutique little cafe offers honest food, friendly service and specialty coffee."

Jo Marazita
Strong Latte

Hash Specialty Coffee and Roasters
Melbourne CBD

The Meatball Wine & Bar
Melbourne CBD

"This unassuming gem on Flinders Lane is my morning retreat before heading into work. Familiar faces greet me when I arrive and they know that on Mondays, my regular latte gets a double shot - I love how they know to do this every week"

Janette, 38
Strong Latte.

12 Cafe on my coffee

White mojo
Melbourne CBD

"I finish a 13 hour shift at the hospital really early in the morning. The atmosphere in the courtyard helps me to relax as the day begins for everyone else."

Alex, 31
Cappuccino

Tom Thumb
Melbourne CBD

"Today the money we make from every coffee is going to the homeless. The organisation is Coffee Smart, and we've had an outpouring of generosity from our customers who are keen to be extra caffeinated this morning! Very philanthropic spirit."

James (Barista)
El Salvador Natural Filtered.

Stokes House
Melbourne CBD

16 Cafe on my coffee

"One Saturday morning, I walked into Dukes with a friend and saw my (now) husband sitting having a casual coffee.
My heart began to race with excitement to see him sitting there. The three of us made plans to check out the Makers Market and go for a walk in the forest the following day. Now, whenever I stop in for a coffee I am reminded of that serendipitous moment."

Caitlin, 28
flat white (and probably a sweet treat)

Dukes Coffee Roasters

Melbourne CBD

Good to go coffee
Melbourne CBD

"What I love the most about Good to GO is the generosity of our customers, whether it be donations for our op-shop, or paying it forward to our clients with a coffee and the atmosphere that Hossier Lane brings to the cafe."

Celeste (Barista and Manager)
Long Black

Collins Quarter
Melbourne CBD

"As the sun rises, the Collins Quarter crew are arriving at work, ready for another busy day. The street lights are all turning off as the coffee machine is coming to life. After seasoning the machine, the Paris end of Collins St is starting to come to life. Caffeine hungry corporates are banging down the door, eager for that magical potion to get the cogs turning."

James V (Barista)
Double Espresso followed by Strong Latte

Rustica Canteen
Melbourne CBD

"If I don't have a coffee today there's no way my boss is going to make it out alive."

James, 34
Long Macchiato with 1

Sketching a conversation near
119 Swanston Street, Melbourne

22 Cafe on my coffee

Sensory lab
Melbourne CBD

"I've been in Melbourne for about 3 weeks now but I have been working as a barista all around the world. I am originally from New Zealand. I aimed for Melbourne because of their coffee reputation, as it is said to be the best in the world. I specifically aimed to work here too."

Marnie (Barista)
Piccolo

Bonnie Coffee
Melbourne CBD

I'm a regular at Bonnie for three reasons. First, the coffee is amazing; velvet and smooth. Second the people who work there are great and always up for a light-hearted chat. Third, Bonnie provides a welcome escape from what can be a repetitive office environment.
I should also mention that they have The Australian pinned up on the newspaper board which is always great. I always recommend Bonnie as the best coffee in Melbourne.

Peter
Long Black

"Where have you bean? At out favourite coffee house, league of honest coffee"

Marcus & Narelle
Flat White & Latte

The League of Honest Coffee
Melbourne CBD

"At Bowery they give you a hershey kiss with your coffee. I would put it in my jacket pocket and it was the best thing on a Friday when you discover the chocolate later on that day."

Stephanie
Flat white
Iced latte if its hot.

Bowery to Williamsburg
Melbourne CBD

Eating a Baguette at Degraves Street,
Melbourne

28 Cafe on my coffee

Kinfolk

Melbourne CBD

"Kinfolk is more than just a coffee shop. Is a place where people want to be at work so it's different to other places. Is more like a family: a weird weird diverse family."

Huk (Volunteer manager)
Cappuccino

Bon a Manger

32 Cafe on my coffee

Little Colin
Melbourne CBD

"Little Colin is called this because we are...
LITTLE.
We keep it simple but make it great.... Coffee.
Food. Chat. Tunes. Just what you need every day
in this glorious part of the CBD."

Vanessa (Owner)
Flat white or two before 7am. Long Black after.

34 Cafe on my coffee

Cento Mani
Melbourne CBD

"The smell of coffee reminds me of my grandfather walking around his farm in Colombia.
It ties me to my most memorable memories and brings me closer to him because he is no longer here. Offering coffee in Australia is a tribute to my grandfather. A Colombian, like many, who dedicated his life working in the countryside".

Diego Reyes (Owner)
Long Black

36 Cafe on my coffee

Degraves street coffee shops
Melbourne CBD

"We come here for the atmosphere, we talk to people, we meet new people, we know everyone, this place its comforting"

"I come here for a different reason: You see that door over there? You must go in there, down the stairs...
A 100 years ago this was different. Underneath us, there is Melbourne's first ever bowling alley, it's meant to be a beautiful piece of art-deco architecture, but is also buried and maybe full of water, incredibly expensive to restore it. Down the stairs I mentioned, there is a toilet with 3 cubicles, two are new, one is original from that era... but that's a story for another day..."

Ro and Mic
Soy Cappuccino & Small Turkish

Patricia
Melbourne CBD

"The main thing for us is getting to know people, is really not that complicated. We have a consistent product but we want to make people happy, wether you work here or come for coffee."

Bowen (Barista)
Filtered Coffee, Milk coffee but mainly Espresso

"Why I go there every morning? Because of the guy with the red lipstick (she smiles). Makes me feel is the right place for me. Great coffee with like-minded people."

Missy (Coolest haircut I've seen)
Latte

Brother Baba Budan
Melbourne CBD

42 Cafe on my coffee

kit espresso

Melbourne CBD

"This one time at KIT, I wasn't having a good morning so Andrew offered me a brownie & taught me how to make a double espresso on their La Marzocco coffee machine.
I sat down and we talked and laughed over an awesome coffee.
Kit is the place I go to for lots of laughs, great coffee, and wonderful staff."

Steve
Double espresso

Verandah Cafe
Melbourne CBD

"Nestled under the Baptist Church's grand Corinthian columns at Collins Street's 'Paris end', the cafe provides a place of rest and welcome in the heart of the city. Serving great coffee and staffed primarily by volunteers, the cafe is an expression of the church's commitment to hospitality in the neighbourhood."

Ptr. Simon
Flat White

Little Rogue

Melbourne CBD

A heavy, blue door which greets you with a little jingle. You feel a warm embrace as you enter this little space – tucked away in one of Melbourne's hidden laneways. No fuss, no clamour… just some seriously good beans from growers around the world. And the tastiest milk coffee I've had too!

Here at Little Rogue nobody shouts your name, but hands you your order with a smile. Their confidence in what they do is well earned. Shhh…don't tell anyone how good this place is!

Julia
Latte

The Little Den

Melbourne CBD

"Love the place, I've been here a couple of times. There's books in the shelves and good coffee. Reminds me of good old days in Fitzroy, big café culture but inner culture. Laidback and free. Now the phase of life is too fast.
In this lane although a decade and half ago me and a friend would sit down here all day, in a little café, and chill out. No tourists. This place was undiscovered. The hipsters, artists, techno crew, would party around the city and the next morning they would all be sitting smoking having coffee. They made this lane popular."

Arris
Latte

48 Cafe on my coffee

Centre Place is my favourite place in the city.
You go there at lunch time when the winter's sun veil
dances within the vapours from the kitchens and by
tunes of the grass roots buskers. Its magical.

50 Cafe on my coffee

Traveller Coffee

Melbourne CBD

"We have a strong regular client base, its like coming and hanging out with you know, good mates. Drink a little coffee, have a chat
Makes working here feel like a community."

Trei and Laura (Baristas)
Double Espresso and Batch Brew

Cup of Truth
Melbourne CBD

I had ten customers in the shop and we were joking and laughing about each other's porn name (...that is, your first pet name plus first street name). A regular customer - an older guy - was walking by, so for some laughs I thought I'd throw him the questions...
Me: 'Hey mate, did you have a pet when you were young?'
Him: 'Yeah I did, silly lab called Mac....'
(Trying to contain our laughter)
I proceeded to ask him...
Me: 'What street did you live on when you had Mac?'
Him: 'It wasn't a street it was WANGO crescent'

So every time he popped in for a coffee I would address him as Mac Wango.

Courtney (Barista)
Espresso

3 little monkeys
Melbourne CBD

"The girls at three little monkeys illuminate Centre Place alleyway, making my morning coffee an even better experience. They are charming and polite and make amazing coffee."

Charlie
Medium Vanilla Latte

Pellegrini's

Melbourne CBD

"Sisto Malaspina grabbed this cup, looked at it closely and with a slight smile on his face he said: -"You know what you have to do?, you have to erase the joy bit from the window, that's just temporary signage, you have to show the Vittoria Cafe sign that we always have. Then you ought to send this cup to Vittoria". Then he tapped his forehead as in saying "thinking it through boy!". While I drew this cup Sisto went outside (it was a cold afternoon) and spent a few minutes with me, he told me about Pellegrini's and how much effort he put into the business.
This man had the biggest charismatic personality in this little big city of ours. He was happy to share his wisdom and charisma with everyone.

Sisto, I am sorry I didn't change the word Joy for Vittoria, because Joy was what you brought to us whenever we visited Pelligrinis and encountered your smile."

58 Cafe on my coffee

Cycle to a gig

South of Johnston

Collingwood

"We wanted to take Meli somewhere physically comfortable as she was heavily pregnant with baby no1. We loved the funky hipster and slightly nostalgic fitout. Plus we knew they had snuggly seating next to the cozy fireplace which we were lucky enough to score on the day! Ps. Alfie would only take us where the coffee was great and I would only take you where the chai was great!"

Penny and Alfie
Soy Chai & Espresso

"We love coming here before heading to the MCG for football. We go to all the Hawks games and finals and have queue in the MCC line with our little daughter but she loves it. We are very lucky!".

Chan-Tha
Soy Latte for everyday
Cold Brew for warmer days

Richmond

62 Cafe on my coffee

Auction Rooms
North Melbourne

"I was pregnant, and maybe over emotional. I wept of joy when I tasted my brunch, following a tear or two for my coffee."

Melissa, 35
Soy Latte

De Clieu
Fitzroy

"I don't want to be the kind of person who orders a tumeric latte but that's wo they make me. Luckily when I need the real deal they nail that too. And yes, I will have one of those pastry treats from the counter and thank you for asking. I grab the window seat in the sun every time. Not simply near the window, the window itself is the seat. I let my legs dangle into the street."

Jess
Long black as of today

Gertrude Street has a tram stop, an art shop, galleries, cafes, curious shops and book retailers.
What else do you need?

Archie's all day

Fitzroy

"First trip away with our six month old Lana, it was hectic. Running late and unable to find parking space. Got here in the end, and yes finally, a strong latte!"

Nugie, 30
Strong Latte

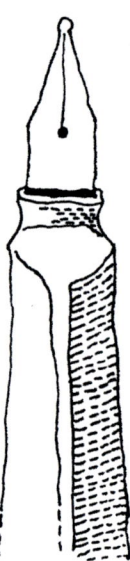

70 Cafe on my coffee

"Roasting: is it an art or is it science?
As a roaster, this is a question I often get.
My short reply is that it was once wholly artisan's craft.
With the addition of modern technology, the science
has become more prevalent.
But underlying remains the inherent human skill.
As in all art, irrespective of its form.

The aim is to provide sensory pleasure, food for
thought, conversation and ultimately, enjoyment"

John (Roaster)
Long Black

Merlo Coffee

Queen Victoria Market

Common Ground
North Melbourne

72 Cafe on my coffee

Dr. Morse Bar & Eatery
Abbotsford

"I don't come here just for coffee, I come to have a chat and be myself! The catch up on a monday morning after a big weekend is like therapy"

Nanna, 33
Strong Flat White

Grub Food Van
Fitzroy

"Full of dirty hipsters."
"Our dog loves it."
"Awesome, I mean really good."
"Male waiter with attitude spoilt the experience somewhat."
"It's funky and a real find in the city."

Grub's customers

There is a rise of bicycle commuting in Melbourne.
It's forgiving topography makes it easy to be anywhere.
The result: the popularity of local-designer bike culture
an hybrid bike-coffee shops.

The glass Den
Coburg

Three Bags Full
Abbotsford

Two Birds
Collingwood

Most Melbournians pick their coffee at 9:30am.
Latte seems to be the preferred drink for the majority.

Dexter Melbourne
Preston

Rupert on Rupert
Collingwood

Industry Beans
Fitzroy

"I come in to Industry Beans a few times a week for a Fitzroy Iced – it's my afternoon treat! I get to sit in their beautiful courtyard surrounded by coffee trees, locals and doggos. The staff are uber friendly and super relatable, no sign of any too-cool attitude here. It's the coffee and the team that keep me coming back."

Sara
Fitzroy Iced

Mina.no.ie
Collingwood

86 Cafe on my coffee

"I love to brunch here... the staff area is great and the menu always has something new to try. Check out the space at the front, it feels out-side, but it's inside."

Sef, 35
Single shot long black, one sugar

MJR Tom
Collingwood

S.T.R.E.A.D
Collingwood

Lune Croissant

Fitzroy

I always go to Lune for the croissant. The best!
I also enjoy watching them making such precise and crafted pastry.
The first time I went, I bought a few croissants extra for takeaway. They survived the trip to Sydney, back home and on my bike (sitting on my bike rack) to work on the next day!

Cristina, 33
Latte

While drawing this on Smith Street a woman waiting for the tram spoke to me on how she misses her son who is overseas. Now everytime I see the Patersons Building from the tram stop I think of her.

Market Ln.

Queen Victoria Market

"As a designer, the window storefront of this cafe looked like a specialized shop and the people sitting inside blended beautifully with the rest of the streetscape, all cute Melbourne designer shop fronts.. Now, these shops have closed but luckily for me, Market Ln did not go too far".

Melissa
Latte

The Kitchen at Weylandts
Abbotsford

" I love PMC because the tunes are always banging, the coffees are always sensational and the crew is genuine. It's so cool when a customer remembers a coffee from the year before and is pumped to see it back on the menu. We are pretty passionate about our relationships, and to see the impact of that from farm to customer is really something special."

Sam, 28
Filter

Proud Mary
Collingwood

Seven Seeds Specialty Coffee

Carlton

"I study at Melbourne Uni. I love coffee but is coffee who is addicted to me. I also come here every day because of the soup, I love it!"

Jake, 25
Flat White Almond Milk

100 Cafe on my coffee

Drop by the market

"Every day I stare at Pardon from across the street where I sit at my desk drinking my delicious Pardon takeaway coffee. Every now and then when I look over I catch the eye of the barista and we exchange a smile, a laugh or wave.
Makes my day."

Caitlyn, 30
Almond latte

PARDON Coffee
Prahran

Uncommon.
Windsor

Parlour Diner
Windsor

Bitter End
Prahran

Abacus

South Yarra

"I live near by and come by for coffee most days. Baristas are always friendly and up for some silly banter."

Thomas, 25
Magic

108 Cafe on my coffee

Miletos
Windsor

The Windsor End of Chapel Street comes with all types of colours, shapes and sizes of where to eat, drink and have coffee. You gotta love it.

Jasper, 40
3/4 Latte

Pietro e Paolo
South Melbourne

"Thanks to this beautiful courtyard I can enjoy my coffees for longer time. Our toddler will play here for hours!"

Julio, 36
Latte

Toorak Cellars

Armadale

"This isn't a wine bar, it's a community centre.
For 9 years, this is where the neighbourhood has come to eat, drink, laugh and live.
Wether your looking for love, celebrating friendships current or past, or just checking in with yourself over a glass of Burgundy, 'The Cellars' is YOUR Wine bar."

Geoff, 50
Espresso

"I come here every time I come shopping because it's convenient and I live around the corner. In each market in melbourne theres a market lane coffee and it's a nice atmosphere. I also love their coffee. Its consistent."

Steph
Strong Latte

Market Lane Coffee
Prahran Market

Coffee roasting at Market Lane, Prahran Market.

"We enjoy watching the roasting process while we drink our lattes after buying our vegetables."

Sally and Pete
x2 Flat whites

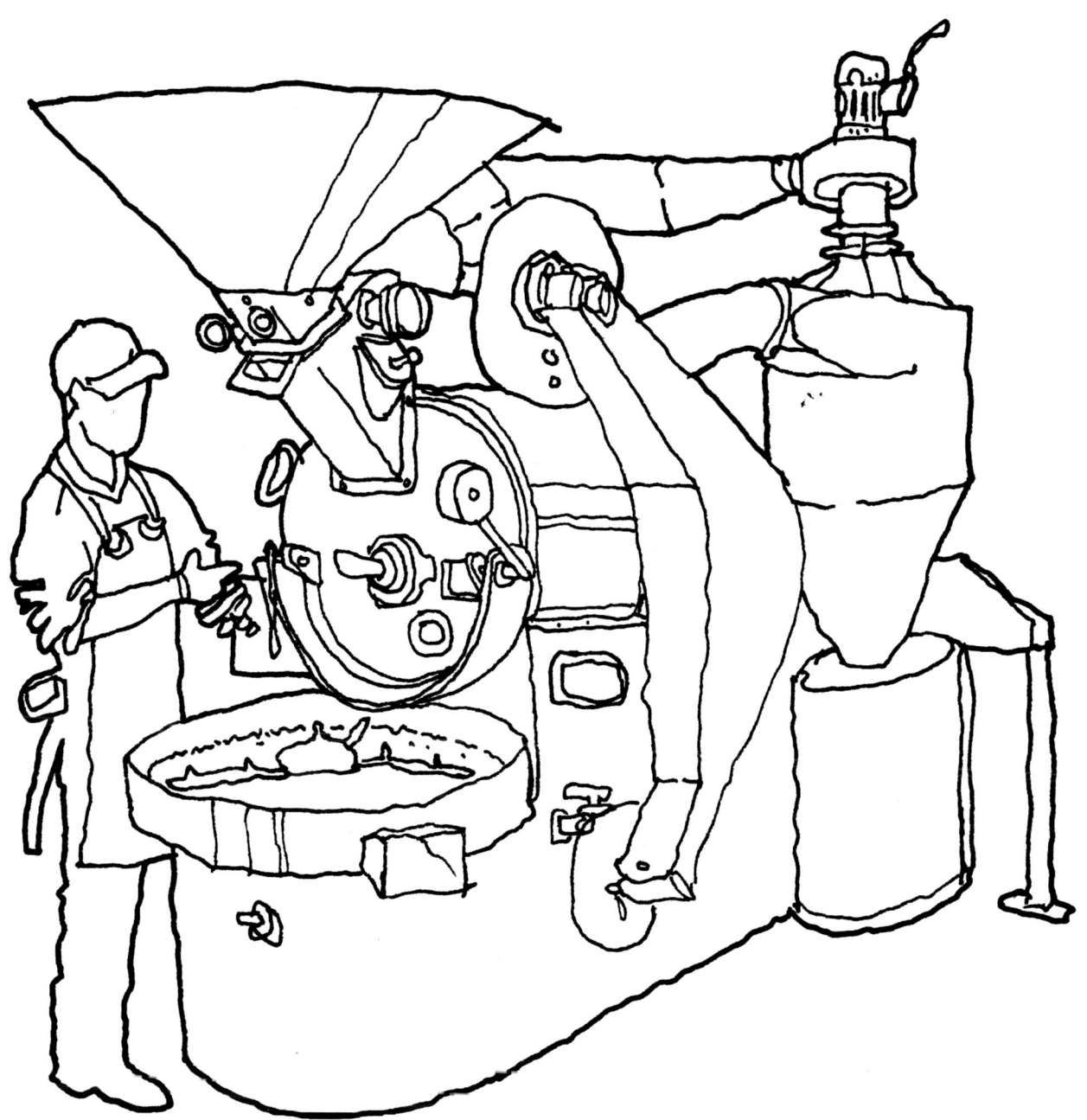

Mammoth
Armadale

Soldier on

Windsor

St Ali
South Melbourne

"I knew a guy who used to work here, he got me into coffee. Now I come here pretty much every morning on my way to work. This place is very well known you know. St Ali is an institution in Melbourne."

Mel
Strong latte

Montague Park food store
South Melbourne

120 Cafe on my coffee

Rococo Lane
Armadale

"We really enjoy coming to Rococo Lane for our daily delightful caffeine fix and pleasant chats with the owner.

But the gift that keeps on giving are their indulgent take home meals, which I now currently believe my lovely wife has completely forgotten how to switch on the oven, one would say this is a "win win situation" for all."

Andrew & Beth, 71
Cappuccino

Journey Man

Windsor

"I was sitting facing the street on a side table, gleaming in, flat white in my hand, with the distinct J logo on the cup in my peripheral. She said 'We are pregnant!'... so yes, sometimes coffee becomes the last thing on my mind"

Steven, 30
Flat White

She Bangs

Prahran

"A solid anchor in my morning routine. 7 days a week. 365 days. Without fail. This is the best coffee in our little part of the planet. Nothing like it. The sounds. The smell. The sight of street art everywhere. Fiercely loyal."

Erz
Magic Mocha

"These guys have the brew and smiles to get my day started. Always welcoming, top notch coffee & dog friendly - my boy loves this place as well!"

Dougie
Double Espresso

Oscar Cooper
Prahran

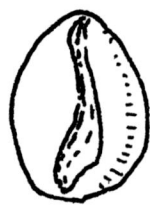

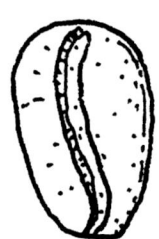

TUSK

Windsor

"I've just come back to Windsor after living in the US for 5 years.
L.A. is the Sahara Desert of decent coffee!
So glad that your still doing what you're doing and you haven't changed a thing for 15 years."

"Good to be home"

Rusty
Long Black

The Anchor on Anchor Place
Prahran

I saw these grinders in a big Coffee shop in the city.
I was drinking a single origin Nicaraguan coffee. It made me
think on the Nicaraguan people, how places in deep struggle still
manage to pick us up with what they produce.

132 Cafe on my coffee

Franklin
Windsor

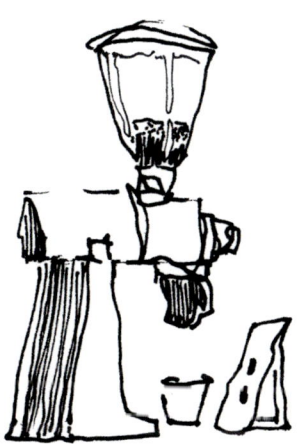

"In a street full of coffee shops they are the best coffee and more importantly make it the way I like to drink it, not the way they think I want it (that goes for food as well, I am a tad odd that way).

Penny, 60 (bookshop owner next door)
Long weak black, warm

Le Petit Prince
Armadale

Fourth Chapter
Prahran

"I make around 20 baby-chinos a day"

Nick (Barista)
Magic

Cooper & Milla's
Armadale

From on High
Prahran

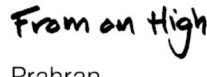

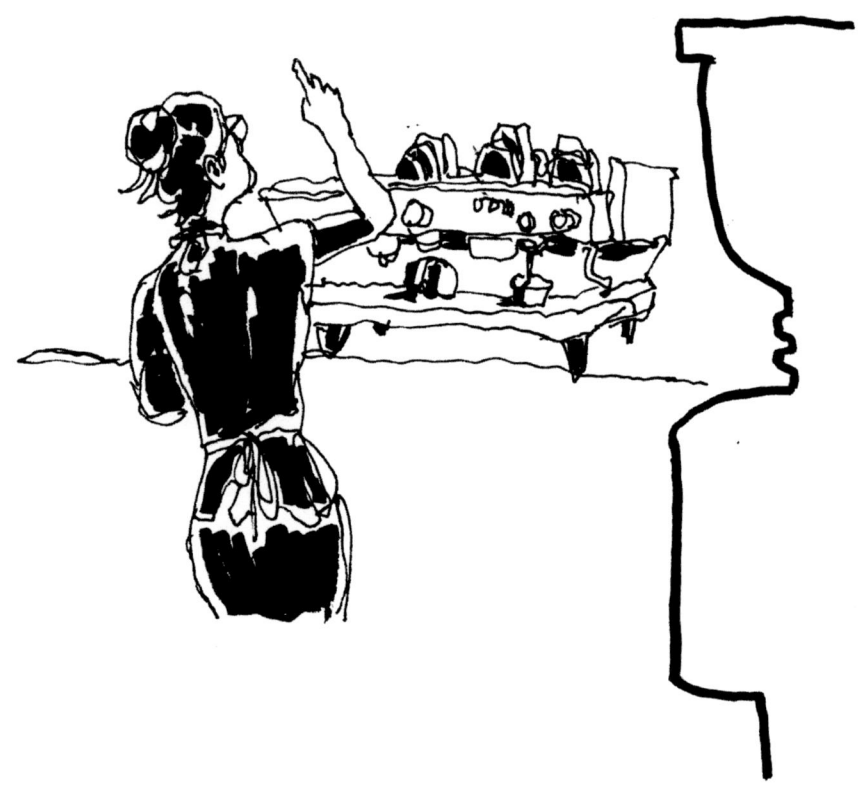

It's not far off

Healthy self co.
Yarraville

"The girls know my order as soon as I walk though the door not to mention what I was up to at the weekend.. !! This cafe truly is a standout for me"

Alex
Long Black

142 Cafe on my coffee

Rudimentary
Footscray

"What a great final stop after a walk around Footscray neighborhood! We love their veggie patch and the idea of converting containers to a cafe. On a beautiful weather day, the outdoor space would be packed with kids and dogs. It is such a place for families and friends! "

Gate, 37
Latte with no sugar please

Oscar Mike
Hawthorn

Cupcake Central
Hawthorn

"Red velvet cupcake and a latte. It's a match made in heaven if you ask me!"

Anita, 37
Latte

Melbournians have made Melbourne
the Coffee capital of Australia

148 Cafe on my coffee

Can I have the lid too?

Drawing a Cafe on My Coffee
by Julio Brenes

Meet you at the city

You might see me drawing around. Please come and say Hi!
I am always happy to meet art lovers and coffee lovers!

Takeaway

Drawing in these cups is my way to recycle. But in essence, is also my drawing-self taking over to draw that place out.
This project would have never happened if I didn't have time unplug.
No internet and no smartphone distractions. (Although, some cups were filmed and they are at drawthatout.com).
So try to be more creative, leaving your phone behind for long stretches of time and take only your creativity with you (you can also take a coffee on a reusable cup).
Wishing you a happy journey and a creative life.

156 Cafe on my coffee

Julio sketching at Prahran Market
Photo by: Melissa Mena

Latte for...

Each cup at the Cafe on my Coffee Book is drawn by the author, Julio Brenes.
Originally from Costa Rica, Julio has been drawing for many years and he took special interest in drawing on coffee cups in 2015. The connection seemed logic for him as someone who loves sketching and sitting at Melbourne's cafes.
Julio moved to Australia in 2008 and after living in Sydney and Canberra he moved to Melbourne with his wife in 2014.
He is now drinking coffee and drawing with his young family at every new Melbourne cafe.
He goes back to his favourite cafes often, when his 2 under 2s sons sleep.

You can find more of Julio's work at www.drawthatout.com
We thank you for your support, cheers to you!

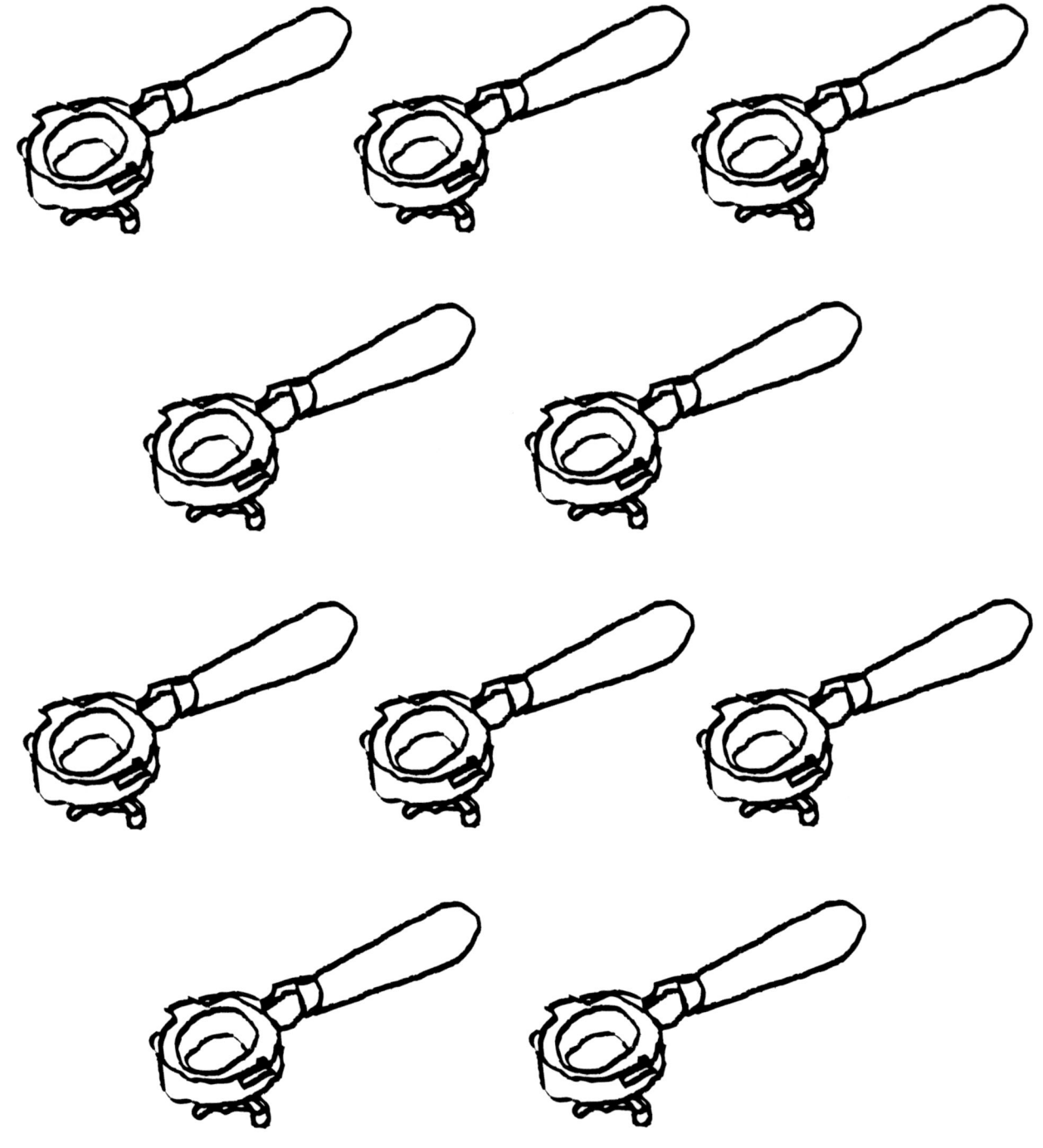

Made in the USA
Middletown, DE
10 April 2025

74054462R00097